Anything Other Than Naked

ANYTHING OTHER THAN NAKED

A guide for men on how to dress properly for every occasion

Glen R. Sondag

Langdon Street Press

Langdon Street Press
212 3rd Avenue North, Suite 290
Minneapolis, MN 55401
612.455.2293
www.langdonstreetpress.com

ISBN-13: 978-1-936183-83-8
LCCN: 2010938401

Cover Design & Typeset by Nate Myers

Cover Photo © 2010. All rights reserved - used with permission.

Printed in the United States of America

DEDICATION

*T*o my mother, Adelia "Dale" Sondag, who clearly influenced my love affair with apparel. At age ninety-nine she is still going strong, dressed every day in a skirt and blouse, or a dress, accessorized with a colorful brooch, and a pair of high-heeled shoes. Is there another woman on the planet who has worn high-heeled shoes every day for over seventy years? (My mother mowed the lawn in heels!) In my lifetime, I've seen my mother wear a pair of slacks only once— she was up on a ladder painting the back of the house. Modesty dictated her choice of apparel.

FOREWORD

*T*his piece presents the thoughts and ideas I've shared with my four adult sons on choosing a wardrobe, along with some dos and dont's for dressing smartly and appropriately. It started out as a checklist of things for them to consider and then morphed into something more. I hope the insights offered are helpful and perhaps cause you to think about how you present yourself when you are anything other than naked.

ACKNOWLEDGEMENTS

I want to thank several people, all of whom help me look my best. They include shirtmaker Frank HeeKang from Riddle McIntyre, Inc., who for the past thirty-one years has made my shirts; Larry Hirsh from Tom James Co.; and tailor Larry Ilirjan of Ilirjan Dry Cleaners.

Special thanks to Les Hale for his invaluable evaluation and to Kelly Brookhouse Lulis, who helped me organize this book, assemble the art, and prepare it for publication. To Lynda and Jim O'Connor of O'Connor Communications who guided me through the process of getting published, and lastly, to my loving wife Sue, who tells me every day that I look nice.

CONTENTS

INTRODUCTION

s a young boy, a familiar scene was repeated many times in the evening at our small home in New Ulm, Minnesota, in the early 1950s. My father would be watching TV from his favorite chair while my mother knelt on the living room floor cutting a McCall's dress pattern from fabric spread out on the carpet. I would help as she precisely cut the material with her pinking shears. I learned then what admittedly most boys never had any reason (or desire) to learn: the difference between wool, cotton, rayon, and silk (polyester hadn't been invented yet).

Mother made anything and everything if there was fabric involved, from wedding dresses to draperies. She even covered women's hats and shoes with fabric. Dad surely didn't mind, as Mother made virtually all her own clothes—save for her girdles. Mother sewed so much that she actually wore out a sewing machine every few years. She looked forward to getting a new, better, and faster Singer sewing machine like most men looked forward to their next new car.

Over the years, I often talked with Mother while she sewed, and from those conversations I learned about fabric, tailoring, fit, and clothing construction. Every Easter, Mother made me a new sport coat to wear to church. I'll always remember the red blazer I wore to Easter Sunday Mass at age ten, complete with white shirt, black slacks, black tie, and "white bucks" (loafers). I thought I looked as cool as Elvis!

I readily admit that I have liked clothes from an early age, and as I've grown older, my interest in clothes has never waned. While attending graduate school, I worked in a clothing store, only to spend every dime I made on new clothes. Later, while in the military, I often thought to myself that I could never make a career of the Air Force, as I did not like wearing the same thing to work every day. In my early days as a stockbroker, I took particular pride in always looking better than I could afford to look. Thousands of dollars and decades later, I have some definite opinions and observations about men's clothing, and how best to dress for both casual and professional occasions.

Let me begin by saying that most men don't dress very well—some because they simply don't care how they look, others because they have no sense of color or style. Many more rely on others to pick out their clothes for them—people who don't have much more fashion sense than they do! Having said this, how do I know that I dress well? Primarily because I have been the recipient of compliments from both men and women for as long as I can remember. I guess you could say that I'm a "straight guy" blessed with a "queer eye."

The size and scope of your wardrobe should be in direct proportion to your interest in clothes, your finances, and your need for both business and casual wear. If you like to look nice in any circumstance, then everything in your wardrobe matters—from your suits to your shoes. My purpose here is to offer tips and commentary on what to include in your wardrobe, and how to look your best.

You may be asking, "Are there really any rules of dress that must be followed anymore? Who makes the rules, anyway?" You can be forgiven for thinking that there are no rules or conventions when you observe most men's proclivity for dressing poorly. For example, I always thought that at least one rule was inviolate: Always wear black socks with a tuxedo. This belief was shattered some years ago when I stepped into an elevator at the Waldorf Astoria hotel with a former professional football player attired in a tuxedo, finished off with white athletic socks and white Nikes with the laces untied. I guess he was going for the sporting look.

The definition of "modern," or what is considered to be in style, changes over time. Men no longer wear spats, waistcoats, or top hats. Details like coat length and lapel and necktie width also have changed over time. This is not to suggest that every time popular styles change you need to revamp your entire wardrobe. It does mean, however, that you should be both mindful of and willing to make subtle changes in your wardrobe over time.

As you get older, your tastes, too, likely will change. Nothing brings this home more readily than looking at old photos of yourself. What you found stylish at age twenty-five probably looks nothing like what you find, or will find, acceptable at age fifty-five.

Source: Vanity Fair

This past decade has borne witness to a pronounced move to casual attire worn in more situations. There was a time not long ago when men always wore a tie with a suit, and a sport coat and jeans was not considered an acceptable combo. We should not be surprised by such changes when you have the likes of Hugh Hefner spending both his waking and non-waking hours in silk pajamas. Then there is Apple founder and inventor, Steve Jobs, who routinely launches new products wearing denim jeans and a black mock turtle.

Having noted that, here are nontheless some basic tenets for dressing properly:

Proportion. Wear clothing that flatters your physique. For example, a portly fellow ought not to wear a shirt or a sweater with horizontal stripes, nor a bold, plaid suit. Learn to wear what looks good on you.

Color. Wear colors that complement your complexion. One of the best ways to determine your "best" colors is to pay attention to the colors you're wearing when people compliment your attire. If you are heavyset, dark colors are going to be more flattering on you than light colors. People with sandy-colored hair or a reddish complexion will generally look good in brown, tan, or beige tones. If you have salt-and-pepper hair, anything gray is very flattering.

Speaking of color, some men are colorblind—between 5 and 8 percent, depending on what study you read. There are different kinds and degrees of color-vision deficiency. Chances are that if you have colorblindness, you cannot perceive shades of red or green. The next time you have an eye exam, ask your practitioner whether you have this condition. If so, then you may be combining the wrong colors of suit, shirt, and tie. Ask someone else to make your color choices for you instead. Just be certain that person isn't color blind as well.

Occasion. Dress for the occasion. Have you ever noticed how women always seem to know what to wear, where? That's because they talk to one another ahead of time to be certain that they're properly attired. But how often has a guy called you before attending an event to ask, "Hey Bob, are you going with your blue blazer or your olive green gabardine suit tonight?" We men are pretty much left to figure it out for ourselves. So, if in doubt, dress *up*, not down. It's a much better feeling showing up to a summer lawn party in a summer-weight sport jacket and open collar shirt when everyone else is in shorts and polo shirts, than appearing in sandals and tie-dyed T-shirt when everyone else is in jacket and tie. If you are in a business setting, never dress more casually than your client.

Today, "business casual" is quite common in the workplace, meaning no need for a coat and tie. This leaves considerable leeway in what to wear to work. You'll never go wrong wearing a pair of wool trousers. Cotton slacks are okay, but they won't look as crisp at the end of the day. Tan, navy blue, or gray wool gabardine slacks are a particularly good look for most men, and they're versatile, too, being available in both summer- and winter-weight fabrics. But by all means, avoid wearing denim to the office. Although jeans are an indispensable part of every man's wardrobe, they simply are too casual for the workplace and do not fit any definition of "business casual." That includes wearing a sport jacket and blue jeans together—okay for traveling, but not in the workplace.

As for shirts, any long-sleeved collared shirt will do fine; just be sure it doesn't look like something you'd wear to the beach. Polo style (golf) shirts are not considered acceptable business casual attire. Sweaters are always okay: cotton in the summer, wool or cashmere in winter. With business casual, you can even get by with more colorful socks than the traditional plain black or brown. Paul Stuart (www.paulstuart.com) carries a great selection of colorful socks.

If in doubt about how "business casual" is interpreted at your place of work, take your lead from your male superiors. If their idea of business casual is a sport coat and tie, you won't go wrong by wearing the same.

There are many other occasions when you don't have to guess what to wear—the invitation, or event announcement, tells you what is appropriate. You will see words like, "Black Tie" or "Cocktail Attire" or perhaps "Business Attire." You need to understand what terms like these imply if you are going to be properly dressed for the occasion. The first one, "Black Tie," means that the host is asking you to attend wearing a tuxedo. If you don't have a tux, or don't wish to rent one, wear a dark suit with a white shirt and tie.

"Semi-formal" is yet another term you may see on an invitation. This term calls for wearing a dark suit and tie, not a sport jacket. Next in order is "Business Attire," which suggests you wear a suit and tie. "Cocktail Attire" has come to mean a suit or a sport coat with tie. The next notch down in formality is "Business Casual," meaning a sport coat, with or without a tie, or just a collared shirt or mock turtleneck. Last on the list is "Casual Attire," which has come to mean slacks, jeans, or shorts, with a polo shirt or collared shirt, or even a T-shirt.

SUITS

*I*n the hierarchy of apparel, the suit reigns supreme. Here is your chance to look like a million bucks. How many suits does a man need? Very few if business casual is the norm where you work, but, generally, six suits will serve most men well. At a minimum your wardrobe should include a navy blue solid and a gray solid suit, plus a blue chalk or pinstripe, and a gray stripe suit. If you live in a suit, you can easily add scores more in a variety of patterns and colors.

Finding the right suit for you requires understanding how various features contribute to the overall look, feel, and fit. If you are very tall and slender, avoid vertical stripes. If, on the other hand, you are burly, vertical lines will make you look slimmer. So will wearing trousers with no cuff and no flaps on the pocket of the suit jacket. If you are heavyset, don't wear a double-breasted jacket. Short men should avoid block patterns. Very simply, if you are tall, you need to break up the vertical line, whereas men who are short need as long a visual line as possible.

Shoulders. When choosing a suit, look first at the cut of the shoulder. Is it a square shoulder or rounded? Men with slight builds look best in a square-shouldered jacket, as it makes them look stronger. On the other hand, men with big shoulders should opt for a jacket with a rounded shoulder. Tall men, and men with wide faces, benefit from a suit with a wide shoulder cut.

Jacket Front. The traditional suit jacket is single-breasted with either a two-button or three-button front. Most men look best in a two-button jacket. Taller men can wear a three-button style, which is cut about an inch longer than the more traditional two-button style. The rule about buttoning your jacket is simple and easy to remember: never button the bottom button, and always button the one above it. Buttoning the top two on a three-button jacket is optional, albeit I think the jacket drapes better if the top two are secured. Unfortunately, you see this rule violated quite often, and by people who should know better.

Double-breasted jackets are another choice, although not as popular in the United States as they are in Europe. They do look elegant, but only tall and slender men should wear them. A double-breast-ed jacket should be buttoned when standing, as it doesn't drape well when left open. Open the jacket when sitting. If you choose a double-breasted jack-et, wear trousers with cuffs, unless the trousers lack pleats. In that case, the slacks should not be cuffed. Do not wear a button-down collar shirt with a dou-ble-breasted jacket.

Double-breasted Jacket

Pockets. There are three types of pockets on jackets: flap, patch, and besom. Most suit jackets have the standard pocket with flaps (which should never be tucked in the pocket). Sport jackets will have either a flap pocket, or the more casual patch pockets that look sewn on. The besom pocket is only visible as a slit with no flap, commonly found on tuxedos, but also on some suit jackets. The besom pocket is a better choice for a man who is short, as the lack of a flap makes for a longer visual line.

Vents. Jackets come with a center vent, side vent, or no vent at all. The traditional investment banker suit likely will have a center vent, as will sport coats and blazers. European-style suits more often have no vent. Double-breasted jackets should have side vents or no vent. The drawback to no vent on any kind of jacket is that when the jacket is buttoned, it won't "give" when you reach to put your hand in your trouser pocket(s). Likewise, it can be constricting on portly men. The side-vented jacket is less popular but is very flattering on many men (albeit not on men with large hips) and is very comfortable when moving about.

Center Vent   Side Vents   No Vent

Length. The length of your suit jacket is critical to a good-fitting suit. You want the jacket to cover your buttocks and yet give the leg as long a line as possible. According to Alan Flusser, author of *Dressing the Man* (HarperCollins 2002), there are two measurements that apply to gauging the proper length of a suit jacket. The first is fairly simple: with your hands hanging at your sides, your thumb knuckle should align with the bottom edge of the jacket, plus or minus one-half inch. The second is a bit more involved. Ask the tailor to measure the distance from the floor to where the back collar of the jacket joins the coat's body. The length of the jacket should be one half of that measurement. As with the first method, adjustments must be made to account for long legs, a short torso, and other such features unique to you.

Suit manufacturers make their garments in Regular, Short, and Long sizes, and some in Extra Short and Extra Long. If you're 6′2″ or taller, you probably ought to wear a Long; if you're 5′5″ or shorter, a Short may be your best option. A good rule of thumb is for short men to wear a slightly shorter jacket and tall men to wear a longer one. Don't be afraid to have the tailor shorten a jacket if it is too long, but not so much that the lower pocket flaps are no longer in proportion to the jacket's length. Often, the retailer will not offer to shorten or lengthen a jacket, so ask.

Sleeve Length. Another critical measurement is the length of the sleeve relative to your arm length. You want to have ¼ to ½ inch of shirt cuff showing below the edge of the jacket sleeve—presuming that you are wearing a shirt with the proper sleeve length (to be discussed in a later chapter).

Fabric. Most moderately priced men's suits are made of 100 percent wool. Wool doesn't necessarily mean heavy and hot, nor is it appropriate only for the winter months. Wool suits are available in different weights. The cloth is measured in ounces per square yard. The numbers range from seven (high) to fifteen on the low end. Ten to twelve is considered "all season" weight. It makes good sense to have the majority of your suits in a weight that can be worn eight or nine months a year and to have a few more suits for the very cold and warm months.

Wool goes by several different names including worsted, gabardine, tropical, and flannel. Worsted wool is both durable and breathable. Gabardine is also extremely durable and holds a crease well—a nice choice for a summer-weight tan suit. Another choice is flannel, which is loosely woven and made in heavier weights. In addition to wool there is cashmere, alpaca, mohair, camel hair, vicuna (very rare), linen, and silk. Suits containing silk or linen look and feel very nice but wrinkle like crazy. If the silk content is 15 percent or less, you'll be okay. However, 40 to 50 percent silk content guarantees the suit will look wrinkled after the first ten minutes you have it on! The same goes for linen. (Exception: You are Prince Charles and can afford a Savile Row pure silk, double-breasted jacket to wear to the polo grounds.)

Some casual summer sport coats will be made of 100 percent cotton fabric. This makes for a sporty look, but again it will crush and wrinkle more easily than wool. On the label of almost all suits will be listed the fabric's thread count, with typical counts of 70 all the way up to Super 200. The higher the count, the finer and more delicate the fabric, and the higher the price. That is not to say that a Super 200 will wear better than a 70, but it will look more elegant.

A Super 100 fabric is perfectly suitable to wear to the office.

Color. When choosing suits, begin with blues and grays. There are so many variations of these two colors that you could have twenty different blue and gray suits in stripes, herringbone, tweed, solids, glen plaids, checks, windowpane, pin dots, houndstooth, and more. Black suits are a better choice for weddings and funerals than they are for business occasions. Brown suits are good "filler" but should not be a wardrobe staple. Brown can be elegant for men with certain skin tones as President Ronald Reagan readily

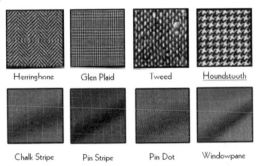

| Herringbone | Glen Plaid | Tweed | Houndstooth |
| Chalk Stripe | Pin Stripe | Pin Dot | Windowpane |

demonstrated, but everything about it—the cut, fit, length, shade, shirt, tie, belt, and shoes—must be exactly right to achieve a professional look. By all means, do not wear a brown suit to make an important business presentation, as you won't look suitably powerful.

When making a presentation, dress in a dark-colored suit and wear your suit jacket with the proper number of buttons buttoned. Don't present in just a shirt and tie if you want to convey power and confidence. If you must buy a green suit, make it your fifteenth suit and avoid wearing it in a business setting, as it will make you look untrustworthy. A tan gabardine suit for summer is a nice change of pace.

Vests. The popularity of vests (worn with a suit) comes and goes. If you wear a vest, the bottom of the vest should cover the waistband of your trousers. Always leave the bottom button unbuttoned.

The Tailor-Made Suit

There are some men who can buy a suit off the rack, have the sleeves altered, the trousers cuffed, and look dapper. There are others who are shaped such that nothing will fit right unless it was made especially for them. There is a third group—those who simply want to have their suits custom made and can well afford to do so.

It is important to understand that there are levels of custom tailoring. There is semi-custom, which amounts to selecting the fabric from a swatch of cloth, then trying on different models of jacket to determine a style preference. The retailer takes a few measurements and sends the information to the manufacturer. Normally the price for this is just a bit higher than what you would pay if you bought the comparable suit off-the-rack. It is called paying an "up charge." Stores such as Nordstrom offer this service, as do many others.

The next is where you purchase the suit from a custom tailor who takes a substantial number of measurements and you pick from either bolts of fabric or swatches. The price range is from about $800 at the low end, to around $2,500.

A truly custom-made suit starts with a fitting by a tailor, after which a paper pattern is made to represent your measurements. The next step in the process involves preparing the linings, cutting the fabric, hand stitching the material, and creating the sleeves and lapels. Everything is done by hand by a seasoned craftsman. You choose from an array of fabric and select the style that you prefer, as well as the color of the lining and the buttons that you like. You will have a second and maybe a third fitting before the jacket is completed to ensure an impeccable fit. The sleeves will have functioning buttonholes with buttons made from animal horn. The jacket will be lined in bemberg (a type of rayon). Savile Row in London is the home of high end custom tailoring. Prices for this level of comfort, elegance, and style start around $3,000 and can go considerably higher depending on the fabric you choose.

No matter what level of custom tailoring you choose, a very sensible idea is to have the tailor make you a navy blue suit with two pairs of trousers. This way your most basic suit will last considerably longer, as slacks typically wear out more quickly than the suit jacket. This is particularly true for men who wear a suit to work but immediately take off the jacket for most of the day.

Men often remark that they loathe shopping for clothes, or at the very least would prefer to spend time doing other things. There is another option: have the clothing company come to you. Tom James Inc. (www.tomjames.com) is a custom clothier offering a full line of suits, shirts, slacks, ties, jackets, etc. One of their representatives comes directly to your home or office to take your measurements and help you make selections. If you are one of those who can't quite figure out what tie to wear with which shirt and suit, Tom James Inc. has solved the problem by manufacturing ties to match its shirt and suit offerings. Tom James Inc. offers merchandise in a wide range of prices to satisfy most tastes and budgets.

If you don't want to spend the money for a tailor-made suit, there are other, lower-cost options such as Jos. A. Bank, which is one of the few places you can buy what are called "separates," meaning they sell suit jackets and slacks separately to accommodate an unusual disparity between your chest size versus your waist. If you are a size 42 in a jacket, the typical off-the-rack suit comes with a 36-inch waist trouser. If you have a 32-inch waist, this presents a problem. (There is usually a six-inch disparity between jacket size and waist size.) At Jos. A. Bank, you can pick out a suit jacket in size 42 and a matching pair of trousers in size 32. What's more, you can purchase two pairs of slacks with the jacket.

Yet another outlet for custom-made suits are the many manufacturers in Hong Kong. Regent Tailors Inc. in Hong Kong is one such company that visits major cities in the United States annually. They set up shop in a hotel for a day or two, and men go to pick out fabrics and get measured for suits, sport jackets, slacks, and shirts. Your garment is manufactured in Asia and sent to you usually within thirty to sixty days. The one drawback to having a suit made this way is that while they take precise measurements, the suit arrives without the opportunity to have it adjusted to fit perfectly as you would if purchasing it at a retail location. Be prepared to spend an additional sum of money to have your local tailor make the necessary adjustments. If you are going to the expense of buying tailor-made garments, they should fit perfectly or you might just as well buy off-the-rack.

Sport Coats

It is a good idea to have at least one sport coat for winter and at least one for summer wear. They are one of the most versatile pieces of clothing in a man's wardrobe. You can wear a sport coat with or without a tie, and a sport coat is right for many occasions when a suit is too much but a shirt and slacks just isn't enough. If you choose to wear a sport jacket without a tie, it's okay not to button the jacket. If you wear a collared shirt with a sport jacket, you have created an appropriate business casual look. In winter a full turtleneck sweater can be substituted for a collar shirt, and at other times a mock turtleneck is acceptable.

At a minimum, consider owning a two-button, center-vent navy blue blazer. It looks great, never goes out of style, and can be worn in just about every setting (save for a job interview) with a pair of gray or tan slacks. Another nice option is a camelhair blazer accented with charcoal flannel slacks. For those who desire the best, buy a 100 percent cashmere blue blazer for the cold months and a lightweight wool blue blazer for summer.

If you want to personalize your blazer, consider replacing the buttons with metal or enamel blazer buttons sporting the logo of your alma mater or some other design holding sentiment for you. A great selection of such buttons can be found in the Ben Silver catalog (www.bensilver.com).

Formalwear / Tuxedo

If you are like most men, you receive more compliments when wearing a tuxedo than at any other time. The fact is, men truly look elegant dressed in a tux. You almost have to work at it to blow it. Johnny Depp and other Hollywood types will, however, manage to do so each year at the Oscars, donning some fashion derivative of this classic ensemble.

The gold standard is a single-breasted, one- or two-button wool jacket with lapels trimmed in satin, and plain-bottom trousers with a matching satin stripe down the outer leg. The tux is worn with a white, winged-collar formalwear shirt, cuff links, studs, a bow tie, cummerbund, suspenders, silk socks, and a pair of formalwear shoes. Be sure to have the "wings" tucked behind the bow tie, and the pleats on the cummerbund should be turned upward.

Source: www.charmingdandy.com

It's okay to substitute a silk formalwear vest in place of a cummerbund with a spread-collar shirt and a formalwear tie instead of a bow tie. Either is acceptable, albeit the latter is not as classic. Tuxedos come in three different lapel styles: a shawl lapel, a notch lapel, or a peak lapel. If you are buying a tuxedo, ask to try on all three. All are elegant and acceptable, with the notch lapel being the most common.

The formalwear rental industry suggests that you rent a tuxedo if you only have occasion to wear formalwear once or twice a year. While this may be true from a dollars and cents standpoint, if you have repetitive occasions in your life that require you to wear a tuxedo (e.g., charity fundraising gala events, award banquets, black-tie holiday parties), then buy a tuxedo. If you choose to rent the tuxedo, at least buy your own winged-collar white shirt, cuff links and matching studs, and a pair of formalwear shoes.

If you are renting, you will likely go to the store weeks before the event to get measured for the tuxedo. Instead of returning to the store the day before the event to pick up the tux, go to the rental store a day or two in advance and try it on. This way, should it need further adjustment, it can be done before you need to wear the garment. Waiting to pick it up the day you need it could result in an ill-fitting jacket or trouser with no time to correct the problem.

TROUSERS / SLACKS

*T*he well-dressed man's wardrobe will contain several pairs of slacks in a variety of styles appropriate to various circumstances. You should consider having two pairs of trousers for each sport jacket. A good wardrobe also includes a pair of slacks in navy blue, black, gray, olive, brown, and tan to wear with shirts or sweaters.

For casual wear, khakis or chinos are a staple item, supplemented with cotton slacks for summer and corduroys for winter. Blue jeans, too, are an essential, but they should fit properly and be comfortable above all else (the best measure of well-fitting jeans is how your butt looks in them). You'll also want to include shorts in your wardrobe, as they're great in warm weather and for any kind of knocking around. Avoid wearing them to formal occasions like weddings or dinner parties, however.

As with suits, there are a number of features that contribute to great-looking slacks:

Length. The length of the trouser has to be *perfect*. If the back edge of the cuff hangs down over the heel, your slacks are too long. If the front edge of the cuff does not touch the top of your shoes, your trousers are too short. The cuff should rest on the top of the shoe just enough to form a slight "break" in front. The general rule of thumb is that the trouser should cover ½ to ⅔ of the shoe. Too long is better than too short.

When having slacks measured by the tailor, you likely won't be wearing a belt. You should therefore hold the top of the waistband with one hand to make sure the pant is at the proper point on your waistline. By the way, watch how you wear your trousers: your beltline should be at, *not below*, your waist. Don't look down while the measurements are taken, as doing so causes the pant to move lower as well. Ask the tailor to angle the back of the cuff slightly lower than the front by a hair. You avoid having too much break that way, and the slack hangs just right on both the front and the back of the shoe.

If you have had the experience of trying on a pair of trousers that fit okay in waist and seat but did not feel comfortable, it was probably because the "rise" was too short. The rise is the amount of room between the crotch and the waistband. Some men can wear a pant with a low rise; the majority cannot. Speaking of a great fitting trouser, try on a pair of Zanella slacks—absolutely divine.

Crease. The crease of the trouser should run right down over the center of the knee. Be sure to hang your trousers by the cuff using pants hangers, rather than draping them over a standard hanger. When slacks are hung vertically, the crease stays fresh and you avoid hanger lines across the middle of the legs. Moreover, you'll find that many wrinkles will magically disappear.

Pants Hanger

Cuffs. Cuffs on dress slacks are the norm; the exception is tuxedo trousers and blue jeans. Cuffs should be 1¼ inches deep. It is acceptable, however, to not put cuffs on trousers that have a plain front (no pleat). Short men should consider wearing trousers without a cuff, as it makes for a longer visual line.

Pleats. Men's dress slacks generally have pleats in the front. A double pleat is most common, but single or triple pleats also are widely available.

Pleats in slacks make them hang nicely, and they flatter most men. A triple pleat will favor a man with large hips.

Single Pleat   Double Pleat   Triple Pleat   English Pleat

Pleats should turn *outward*, toward the pockets. Some slacks are made with what is called an English pleat, meaning that it turns inward. To the casual observer they look the same, and when standing you might not notice the difference, but I guarantee you will when you sit down: the English pleat has the effect of making the front of the slacks puff out when seated, as though you stuffed a wad of cotton down the front of your underwear. If you like the trousers but they have an English pleat, ask the tailor to reverse them. When standing, the pleats should not flare open; if they do, the trousers do not fit you properly. If you see a horizontal crease around the fly, the trousers are too snug.

Not all slacks have pleats, however, and some men look better in slacks with no pleats. It's a matter of personal preference but, having said that, pleated trousers do give you more room when walking or sitting.

Fabric. Fabric choices in slacks include wool (gabardine, flannel, tweed, etc.), cotton, linen, corduroy, and, of course, denim. Since your suit jacket will be wool, by default, so will your suit slacks. Wool slacks look best, drape well, and hold a crease better than other fabrics. When buying wool slacks either as part of a suit or separately, make certain that the front of the slacks are lined in satin to the knee. This extends the life of the trousers by preventing perspiration from soiling the fabric. (A sure sign of a poorly made suit is the absence of lining in the trousers.)

Bermuda Shorts. What a wonderful piece of casual apparel! You might think that the length of Bermuda shorts has remained constant over the years, but you would be incorrect. Just as the basketball shorts that Kobe Bryant wears are longer than those worn years ago by Larry Bird, so have Bermuda shorts undergone a change—they are slightly longer than before.

The appropriate length today is just above the knee when standing erect. If you travel to Bermuda, you will see men dressed in blue blazers, wearing Bermuda shorts and knee-length socks. It seems to look just fine in Bermuda, but somehow doesn't make it in Denver.

DRESS SHIRTS

*E*very man's wardrobe ought to include several dozen long-sleeved cotton dress shirts and at least two shirts with French cuffs. Among your choices are Pima cotton, Sea Island cotton, Egyptian cotton, or the more coarse broadcloth and oxford cloth. (The popular pinpoint cotton is another name for broadcloth.) The first three have a nice sheen, but won't wear quite as well as broadcloth and oxford cloth.

A complete wardrobe will include several white and blue shirts, at least one pink shirt, a cream colored (ecru) shirt, and a few, more soft-colored shirts for variety—striped shirts and blue shirts with white collars are two examples. If the shirt you are choosing has two pockets, it is not a dress shirt. Short-sleeved *dress* shirts are strictly *verboten*.

In addition to dress shirts, you also will want to have several long-sleeved sport shirts for casual occasions: tattersalls, checks, window pane to name a few. The Façonnable brand found exclusively at Nordstrom is outstanding.

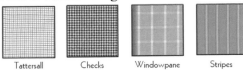

| Tattersall | Checks | Windowpane | Stripes |

The polo style shirt is yet another such essential for summer. Unfortunately, this wonderful and versatile piece of clothing is often worn with a sport coat. The soft polo style collar just does not do justice to the jacket; a button-down collared shirt, or mock turtleneck, looks best with a sport coat.

There are several features to consider in finding a dress shirt that fits you perfectly. Of critical importance is the collar style you choose: it should complement your face. Next, the neck size and sleeve length have to be perfect, which is not easily achieved with off-the-shelf shirts, as both arms likely are not the same length. Lastly, the body of the shirt must be such that it does not appear too tight or too baggy.

Collar Style

When it comes to collar styles, there are a number of choices. The key is to learn which collar works best with the shape of your face. Whichever collar you choose, you want the top of both sides of the collar to touch one another when buttoned; that is to say, there should be no gap between them, so the knot on the tie sits nicely underneath.

Straight-Point Collar. The straight-point collar is best worn by men with an oval or wide face and is the most common collar style. The ideal straight-collar is between 2¼ and 3 inches in length.

Spread Collar. The spread collar is somewhat more elegant and looks best on men with a narrow face. This collar shows off a Windsor knot the best and comes in a variety of lengths and degrees of spread.

Pinned Collar. Still popular today but not as much so as in the past (very popular back in the 1930s), it is called such because a bar or chain is used to connect the collar points. This serves to hold the collar in place and to raise the position of the knot of the tie. Understandably, you need a somewhat longer collar to accommodate the pin.

Tab Collar. The tab collar is an easier alternative to the pinned collar. Instead of relying on a bar or chain to connect the collar points, tabs are attached to each side of the collar and snapped in the middle. Like the pin collar, the tab serves to show off the knot of the tie by raising it just a tad. Both pinned and tab collars look especially nice on men with a long neck.

Button-down Collar. Every preppie's favorite is the traditional button-down collar. This collar certainly is more informal looking than a pinned collar, and should be worn with a blazer or sport coat or when a jacket is worn without a tie. This also is the best collar style to wear with V-neck sweaters, as the tips of the collar will stay under the sweater unlike a spread collar. Every man needs a few of these. It is not the right collar to wear, however, with a dark suit for a formal occasion, nor with a double-breasted jacket.

Neck Size and Sleeve Length

When it comes to shirtsleeves, there is not much room for personal preference, as the cuff should at least pass your wrist bone. Arm length is measured from the middle back of the neck to the wrist with your arms hanging loosely at your sides, not extended. Depending on your suit jacket sleeve length, you may need to adjust the length of your shirtsleeves to ensure that the cuff extends ¼ to ½ inch below the jacket cuff.

Purchasing dress shirts off-the-shelf presents a challenge to getting sleeves that are just the right length. Although ready-made shirts are available in a range of sleeve lengths, if the length you need is not a whole number between 29 and 36 inches, the sleeve will not fit properly. For example, a 35-inch sleeve will be too long, but the 34-inch sleeve too short. If you find yourself in this predicament, by all means buy the longer sleeve and take the shirt to the tailor for adjustment.

Neck sizes are expressed in half-inch increments: e.g., 15 ½, 16, 16 ½, and so on. You should know your neck size as well as your sleeve length. The neck on a shirt should not cause you to turn blue when you button it. Try slipping two fingers between the collar and your neck—if you can do that easily, you have the correct size. If the shirt you are buying is marked as either a small, medium, or large you have another problem, as there isn't absolute uniformity around alphabetical sizing. One manufacturer's medium is another's large. In this situation, you must try on the shirt to determine how it will fit. Don't wait to get home and find that it doesn't fit and then be forced to return it. If you find that it doesn't fit at the store, it saves you a trip and they fold it back up properly. Unfortunately, some stores will not let you unfold a shirt and try it on.

Shirt Body

The shirt body should not be too tight or too loose. If the buttons pull, or the shirtfront shows gaps between the buttons, the shirt is too tight. On the other hand, if you have to tuck mountains of shirt fabric into your slacks and the shirt "balloons out" over your waistband, it is too large. If you have a slight build, look for "fitted" or "tapered" shirts, which are designed for your frame. Cotton shirts may shrink somewhat during the first several washings, so if it is snug when you first try it on, go up one size.

Custom-Made Shirts

Given all the features to consider when selecting the perfect dress shirt, it is no wonder that many men are willing to spend the extra buck and have their shirts custom made. Although more expensive than off-the-shelf shirts, custom-made dress shirts look great because the collar fits right, the sleeves are exactly the right length—even when one arm is longer than the other. If you decide to try custom-made shirts, be prepared to discard all your other dress shirts because you won't want to wear anything else.

Because custom-made shirts are just that—made custom to your body and your preferences—you have the freedom to add or change features to suit your needs and your taste. For example, you can have the cuff made a bit looser on your watch hand so the wristwatch fits comfortably tucked inside the cuff. Or, you may prefer not to have a pocket on the body of your dress shirts, as it makes for a cleaner look.

You can have the shirt made with or without a vertical placket, and with or without a button on the sleeve placket. A vertical placket is the strip of material down the front of the shirt where the buttons are placed. The opening on the forearm of the sleeve is referred to as a sleeve placket. If you wear a shirt with French cuffs, you do need a button on the sleeve placket.

If you like wearing cuff links but don't want to bother with French cuffs, ask your shirtmaker for a convertible cuff. A standard shirt cuff has a buttonhole on the left side of your wrist and a button on the right side. Simply add a buttonhole on the right side as well, next to the button. The result is you can wear cuff links. The button does not show, as it is on the inside of your wrist.

Some men like their shirts monogrammed with their initials. Monograms have traditionally been sewn on the breast-pocket area of the shirt. The trend, however, is for the monogram to appear on the cuff of the shirt. If you prefer to have them on the cuff, put them on the right cuff so that when you extend your arm to shake hands, your initials will show discreetly. Don't ever monogram the collar of the shirt.

Here is a recap of the different choices and combinations for a custom-made shirt.

1. Type of collar—spread, pin, tab, or button-down.
2. If you choose a spread collar, you also get to choose the degree of the spread and the length of the collar points.
3. Front vertical placket or absence of one.
4. Breast pocket or absence of one.
5. White collar and cuffs on a colored shirt.
6. Button cuffs, convertible cuffs, or French cuffs.
7. Your initials monogrammed on the shirt.

All this plus the shirt will fit perfectly in the body, neck, shoulder and sleeve.

TIES

*T*here always is a "right" tie—you just have to look for it. A beautiful tie set against a great shirt with the right collar will properly frame your face and make a great impression. Afterall, the only purpose a tie serves is adornment.

Hands down, the best tie selection on the planet in my estimation is at Neiman Marcus, followed by Paul Stuart and Nordstrom's. These stores carry scores of top brands with varying price points. Brooks Brothers and Jos. A. Banks are alternatives with even lower prices for ties. Fortunately, ties are one item of clothing that always goes on sale. When buying a tie, it's best to have the suit with you.

Neckties. There are neckties that look better with a suit and neckties that look better with a blazer or sport coat. Tie styles best worn with a suit include the elegant and traditional foulard, regimental stripe, and dot styles. Paisley and solid colors are safe bets too.

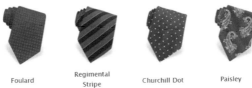

Foulard   Regimental Stripe   Churchill Dot   Paisley

Save the less formal madras, modern print, and club ties for your sport coat or blazer. At the very least, avoid wearing a tie sporting a picture of the Grateful Dead, Mickey Mouse, or NASCAR. Just because they sell them doesn't mean you have to wear them. When shopping for a tie, you may see two of the same tie. If so, take a look at both. One may be blemished or snagged. If the tie has images or large circles, you may find one tie is more symmetrical or centered. Lastly, be careful about wearing a tie that conveys a season other than the present one. For example, don't wear a tie with tulips in November.

Madras   Modern Print   Club

Bow Ties. Wearing a bow tie is a matter of personal preference, albeit 99 percent of men choose to wear a necktie—with good reason, I think. Bow ties are so "right" with a tuxedo, largely because they're shown off by a pleated shirt and cummerbund. They just don't give that same great look when worn with a suit or sport jacket, and they certainly do not project a powerful look, if that is what you're after. If you choose to wear a bow tie, wear a spread collar shirt as opposed to a button-down.

Fabrics. Virtually all ties are made of silk. Nothing looks, feels, or drapes like a silk tie. Occasionally, you'll see a tie made from cotton or wool. Cotton ties are meant to be worn with summer suits and sport coats, and generally speaking, you can get a good knot with a cotton tie. Wool ties can be appropriate for winter wear, but the knot in a wool tie does not hold its shape for more than ten minutes. My advice—avoid both wool and cotton ties.

It should go without saying that clip-on ties are absolutely, positively prohibited. And, by the way, tie clasps and tie tacks went out a long time ago, so if your dad left you his, keep them in a drawer as a remembrance.

When traveling, avoid putting a silk tie in with other items in your luggage, as silk is a delicate material and can easily get snagged or torn. Instead, use a leather or hard plastic tie case or canister to protect your ties. This way your ties won't wrinkle, get damaged, or become soiled.

Length. When standing erect, the tip of your tie should at a minimum brush the top of your belt buckle. At most, it may extend to the bottom edge of your belt buckle. Longer or shorter than that is not acceptable. If your upper body is short, you may find that your ties are too long. The solution is to have your tailor shorten the narrow end of the tie. If your ties are not long enough, buy long or extra-long ties (Nordstrom carries them). Under no circumstances should you tuck your tie into the waistband of your trousers.

Width. The width of men's ties has varied over time, but for the past fifteen years or so, tie width has held fairly constant at four inches across the widest point. The trend appears to be changing to 3¾ and some at 3½. Tie width usually varies with lapel width; wider lapels equal wider ties. Some tie manufacturers produce narrower ties, such as Turnbull & Asser, and Hermes. If you like a tie, but it is too wide, you can always take it to your tailor to be modified to your liking.

When tying a tie, you want to end up with a dimple in the fabric just below the knot. You do this by making sure the material is fed through the knot without bunching, twisting, or creasing. Then, pinch the material below the knot just off center. When you pull down to tighten the knot you end up with a perfectly centered dimple.

After you've knotted your tie, reach around to the back of your neck to make sure the tie is tucked up under your shirt collar. You don't want tie showing beneath your collar. To finish, be sure to run the narrow end of the tie through the loop on the backside of the wide end. If the length is correct, but the narrow end extends below the wide end, simply tuck the narrow end inside your shirt. A permanent fix is to have your tailor shorten the tie.

At the end of the day, untie your tie the opposite way you tied it. Do not simply pull the one end back through the knot, as you will ruin the lining and cause the tie not to hang nicely over time. Be certain your hands are clean when you tie and untie the knot; otherwise, over time, the tie will become soiled, particularly in the knot area, which is handled most frequently.

If you soil a tie, don't take it to just any dry cleaner. Many of them do not have the proper equipment to clean a silk tie.

Tying a Tie

A badly knotted tie spoils the look of your shirt and suit, so it is imperative that you learn to tie a great four-in-hand knot with a dimple, or a half Windsor knot (best with spread collars). Illustrated instructions are provided on the following pages. Practice in front of a mirror over and over again until you get it just right.

How to tie the "Four in Hand Knot"

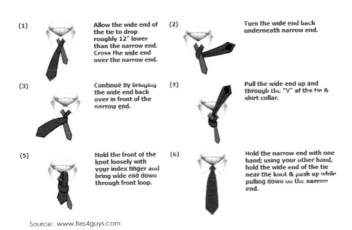

(1) Allow the wide end of the tie to drop roughly 12" lower than the narrow end. Cross the wide end over the narrow end.

(2) Turn the wide end back underneath narrow end.

(3) Continue by bringing the wide end back over in front of the narrow end.

(4) Pull the wide end up and through the "V" of the tie & shirt collar.

(5) Hold the front of the knot loosely with your index finger and bring wide end down through front loop.

(6) Hold the narrow end with one hand; using your other hand, hold the wide end of the tie near the knot & push up while pulling down on the narrow end.

Source: www.ties4guys.com

How to tie the "Half Windsor Knot"

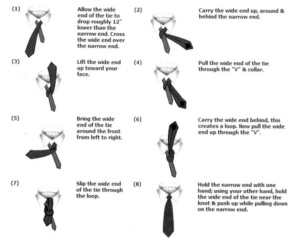

(1) Allow the wide end of the tie to drop roughly 12" lower than the narrow end. Cross the wide end over the narrow end.

(2) Carry the wide end up, around & behind the narrow end.

(3) Lift the wide end up toward your face.

(4) Pull the wide end of the tie through the "V" & collar.

(5) Bring the wide end of the tie around the front from left to right.

(6) Carry the wide end behind, this creates a loop. Now pull the wide end up through the "V".

(7) Slip the wide end of the tie through the loop.

(8) Hold the narrow end with one hand; using your other hand, hold the wide end of the tie near the knot & push up while pulling down on the narrow end.

Source: www.ties4guys.com

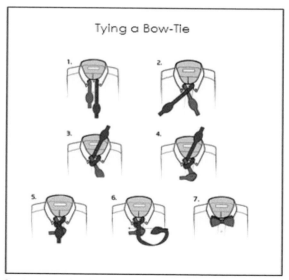

Tying a Bow-Tie

Source: www.quamut.com

"Clothes make the man.
Naked people have little or no influence on society."
Mark Twain, 1835–1910
American humorist and writer

MATCHING SUIT, SHIRT, AND TIE

*I*f you want to look great in a suit, you have to get the combinations right—both the colors and patterns. There are so many tie styles and patterns that it is impossible to make blanket suggestions about what to wear, other than to say that the tie must complement the shirt and suit. Keep in mind that there are colors of shirts that don't look good with a suit or sport coat, but no color is off-limits for ties, save for an all-white tie. If you don't have good color sense, rely on someone who does. But before you rely on the sales clerk to pick your ties, look at how he is dressed. If you don't like his shirt-and-tie combination, why trust him to select yours?

Keep in mind that a suit is made to be worn with a tie, albeit recent fashion trends suggest it is okay not to on certain occasions. If you don't want to wear a tie, I suggest you wear a sport jacket instead. If the occasion calls for a tie, by all means knot the tie to the neck; don't leave the top button of your shirt open with the tie hanging loose. You are not making a fashion statement. Instead, you are saying you like looking sloppy, or your collar is too tight. Whatever the reason, it doesn't look good. Here are some tips for matching suit, shirt, and tie:

- If the suit contains a pattern (e.g. Glen plaid, herringbone, window pane, or stripe) wear a solid color shirt.

- If you want to wear a striped shirt with a striped suit, be certain that the width of the stripes in the suit is different from the width of the stripes in the shirt.

- If you're wearing a very small-checked suit (e.g., Shepherd's check), wear a solid-color shirt, and a tie with a large pattern.

- A solid-color suit with a striped shirt needs a tie that complements both the shirt and suit color.

- If the suit is striped, don't wear both a striped shirt and a striped tie. A plain tie works better.

- Always match a large-pattern tie with a small-pattern suit.

- On a suit with a wide stripe, go with a narrow-stripe shirt with a polka dot tie, or a solid-color shirt with a pattern tie.

- If you are wearing a solid-color suit and a checked shirt, avoid a foulard tie; a club tie or stripe tie works better.
- It's best to choose no more than two patterns for suit, shirt, and tie.

Here is another way to think about matching patterns. Patterns fall into two categories: *major* (the pattern stands out from five feet away) and *minor* (the pattern blends in from less than five feet). Avoid wearing a major-pattern shirt with a major-pattern jacket. I will concede that many in the fashion industry will wear major, major, and major together, however, it is very difficult to do it right. Most don't, and thus the whole thing looks far too busy. Pretty much any other combination will be acceptable.

JACKET +	SHIRT +	TIE =	OK?
MAJOR	minor	MAJOR	Ok
MAJOR	minor	minor	Ok
minor	MAJOR	MAJOR	Ok
minor	minor	MAJOR	Ok
minor	MAJOR	minor	Ok
minor	minor	minor	Ok
MAJOR	MAJOR	MAJOR	NO
MAJOR	MAJOR	minor	OK

If you are looking for some color combinations, here are a few that are sure to hit the mark with a solid navy blue suit:

- Maroon striped shirt with a maroon and white polka dot tie. A white collar and white cuffs is a nice touch. Think about adding a solid maroon pocket square.
- White shirt with blue-green stripes and navy tie with green accents.
- White shirt with blue stripes and a navy/red/white foulard tie.
- Pink solid shirt with a light blue and pink striped or print tie.
- Light gray shirt with a silver/blue tie and gray pocket square.
- Light purple pin dot shirt with a large pattern or print dark purple and blue tie.
- White shirt with red tie.
- Blue shirt with yellow tie. End bullet list here

Dressing for that All-Important Job Interview

Assuming the position you are seeking is not a bartending job at Hooters, you probably want to show up wearing a dark suit, preferably a navy blue solid, with a two- or three-button jacket. Be certain to button all but the bottom button. The trousers should have cuffs, and the bottom front of the trousers must at least touch the front of the shoe. The back of the trouser should not touch the ground when standing erect.

Your best accompaniment is a white or a solid blue pinpoint cotton long-sleeved dress shirt with a spread collar. No dark colored shirts for this occasion. Button-down collars are too casual for wear with a suit. Short-sleeved shirts are absolutely forbidden, even if you are interviewing in the desert. Your shirt will look crisp if you have the laundry add starch to the body, and most importantly, to the collar and cuffs. The cuff of the sleeve should peek out from the suit at your wrist.

You have considerable latitude in the selection of a silk tie. Good taste would dictate a regimental stripe —definitely not your Grateful Dead tie. The knot of the tie matters a great deal. Get in the habit of tying the tie with a dimple in the center of the knot. Make sure the bottom of your tie at least brushes the top of your belt buckle, but does not extend below the bottom edge of the buckle.

Choose a black leather belt, with either a gold or a silver buckle, but make sure the buckle is not something you would see on a rodeo rider. Your socks should be over-the-calf, navy blue or black. Mid-calf socks are acceptable but they must never slip down around your ankles. Select a pair of black lace shoes. Slip-on shoes, tassel shoes, or penny loafers are not okay—they are too casual in this instance.

None of this matters if your hair is not clean and combed, your fingernails are dirty, your tie is soiled, or your shoes are scuffed. You need not make a fashion statement, but you do want to look crisp, clean and professional. The goal is to look like you are CEO material even if you are applying for an entry-level position.

"Good clothes open all doors."
Thomas Fuller 1608–1661
British clergyman and author

SWEATERS

*T*here are numerous styles of men's sweaters—crew neck, V-neck, turtleneck, mock turtleneck, polo, cardigan, shawl, half zip mock, and zippered. Wear what you like and what looks good on you. If you have a short or large neck, you probably should not wear a turtleneck sweater a V neck or crew neck sweater will work better. Horizontal stripes and bold patterns are not flattering on short, heavy-set men; tall men have dibs on these.

Pay attention to whether the sweater has a set-in sleeve (the sleeve attaches to the sweater at the shoulder seam) or a raglan sleeve (there is no shoulder seam; the sleeve continues above the shoulder, tapering gradually to attach at the neckline). Raglan sleeves look better on men with broad shoulders, while set-in sleeves flatter a man with sloping shoulders or a slight build.

Set-in Sleeve   Raglan Sleeve

Before buying a sweater that zips from bottom to top, try sitting down with the sweater fully zipped. These sweaters tend to bunch up when sitting and make you look like you have something stuffed down the front of your shirt.

Cashmere sweaters are simply divine to wear but generally more expensive than wool or cotton. Cashmere is the hair from the soft undercoat of a Kasmir goat. Expect to pay $400 or more for a good, 2-ply cashmere sweater (avoid buying a cheap, thin 1-ply cashmere sweater). Fortunately, you usually can find cashmere sweaters on sale at various times of the year. When cashmere is not an option, wear wool sweaters in winter and cotton sweaters in spring and fall. Merino wool, which comes from Merino sheep, is considered the finest wool, thus making Merino wool sweaters an equally good choice.

Lastly, never hang a sweater on any kind of a hanger, be it wire, wood, or even a padded hanger. Sweaters should be neatly folded when not in use.

OUTERWEAR

*D*epending on the climate you live in, you may need several types of coats and jackets. For starters, you will never regret spending the money for a tan Burberry raincoat. They last for years, are always in style, and can be worn with casual clothes and over a suit (but not over a tuxedo). My preference is their tan cotton/poly, belted model with a zip-out wool liner and a removable wool collar.

On those occasions when your wife is dressed to the nines and you're in a suit, you may want a charcaol grey, navy blue, or black top coat. Cashmere is best, but wool will suffice. Traditional men's top coats have either a single-breasted front with or without a belt or a double-breasted front. Top coats will generally have a center vent. The proper length of a top coat is below the knee but above the calf. A single-breasted, navy blue cashmere top coat is always in style.

In addition to a top coat and a raincoat, you may also want to add a car coat to your wardrobe. They are called such because they are comfortable to wear in a car, as they cover your fanny (mid-thigh length). Waist-length jackets are versatile, but do not wear one over a suit. Add a few jackets in various weights and styles and you will have the right piece of outerwear for every occasion.

If you are inclined to splurge on a piece of clothing, treat yourself to a jacket from Loro Piana (www. loropiana.com). They are hands down the most splendid jackets available anywhere in the world, albeit outrageously expensive.

Winter scarf. You have three choices: cashmere, wool, or silk. Silk scarves are beautiful but lack warmth. Wool scarves are warm but can be irritating on your neck. Cashmere, on the other hand, feels good and provides warmth.

Gloves. If you live in a cold climate, or travel to one, you need at least two pairs of leather gloves: one black pair for wear with black or navy topcoats and jackets, and a brown pair for wear with your beige Burberry rain coat or brown jacket.

Hats. While you rarely saw a man wearing a hat these past twenty years, they are showing up in stores again, particularly the casual 1½-inch wide brimmed model. Called a "trilby," this hat is soft brimmed and worn with casual apparel. Not a mandatory piece, to be sure.

Umbrellas. Most men don't mind a little rain, but who wants to get soaked going to work or to a business or social occasion? There are times when an umbrella is called for. I suggest you buy three collapsible umbrellas—the kind that fit into a briefcase. Keep one in your car, another at home, and a third at the office. One of them will come in handy several times a year. Tumi makes a decent one and Davek makes an outstanding one. If you are prone to losing them, the $10 variety at discount stores will serve the purpose.

BELTS

*B*elts are underrated. The wrong one can actually detract from your overall appearance. For starters, the color of your belt should always match the color of your shoes. If your shoes have a buckle or other adornment, your belt buckle should also match.

Your wardrobe should include at least four leather belts: two black, one brown, and one cordovan. One of the black belts should have a silver buckle, and the second one a gold buckle. The brown belt should have a gold buckle. A cordovan belt can have either. You also may want to consider a reversible belt for travel—black on one side and brown on the other. For casual wear, it is nice to have a few cloth or braided belts in the closet for blue jeans, casual slacks, and shorts. Fortunately, belts often go on sale.

Standard width for belts is 1¼ to 1½ inches. Don't get cute and buy a skinny belt, or one that is so wide it doesn't fit easily through the belt loops. Belt length comes in two-inch increments (e.g., 30, 32, 34, 36, etc.); the appropriate belt length is one size larger than your waist size. For example, if you have a 34-inch waist, buy a 36-inch belt. This rule of thumb has less to do with the possibility that your waistline may expand over time, and more to do with the fact that the belt end (or "toe") should end up between the first and second belt loops when buckled.

With business attire, avoid a belt with a large buckle, as it will draw the eye to the belt instead of where it should be. However, large buckles are okay with jeans.

My guess is that like most people, you put your belt on the same way every day, either left to right, or right to left. You've also probably noticed that after a while, your belt is bowed in the middle. If you hold the belt vertically with the buckle at the top, you can see how the belt bends in one direction. To avoid this, try alternating how you put your belt on—from the left one week, from the right the next. This will keep your belts straight, or nearly so, which in turn will prevent sagging or bunching of your waistband in back. You can further prolong the life of your belts by hanging them on a belt hanger; the kind with hooks that rotates will make finding the right belt fast and easy.

SHOES

*I*f there is one sure way to know if a man cares about his appearance, it is how his shoes look. If they are dull, scuffed, or badly worn, a $5,000 suit won't save you. Believe it or not, your shoes are one of the first things people notice.

Mens shoes come three ways: a laced shoe, a shoe with a strap (monk strap), and a slip-on shoe (loafer or tassle). If you wear a suit, you need a good pair of black, brown, and cordovan laced shoes, preferably in a cap toe, wingtip, or oxford style. With proper care this shoe will last for years and never go out of style. Best of all, you'll feel like a CEO when you wear them. (They've been in style so long that your grandfather probably had a similar pair of oxfords.)

Wingtip   Cap Toe

Oxford   Patent

Loafer   Tassel Slip-on

You also will want to have a black and a brown pair of dress slip-on shoes that you can wear with a sport coat and business casual attire. Penny loafers are considered casual shoes and should not be worn with a suit, though a slip-on has come to be an acceptable alternative to a laced shoe. Shoes with rubber soles are never acceptable with a suit or sport jacket. Suede shoes and two tone shoes are acceptable to wear with a sport coat but not with a suit.

If you have reason to occasionally wear a tuxedo, you will want to buy a pair of black patent leather shoes to wear strictly with formalwear. They'll be a much more comfortable fit and more hygienic than rented shoes. A laced shoe or a slip-on are equally acceptable for formalwear.

The king of all shoe stores is Nordstrom—they carry numerous brands and have a couple of good shoes sales each year. If you really want to indulge yourself, however, try a pair of John Lobb shoes from England, available through Nieman Marcus. Paul Stuart also carries a nice line of English shoes, and Italian maker, Bontoni, makes a splendid shoe.

I highly recommend you own a pair of genuine shell cordovan shoes (as opposed to cordovan-colored shoes). There are only a few manufacturers of these shoes, which wear like iron, look great, and are wonderful for traveling because they can be worn with black, navy, tan, and brown—any color suit or slacks. Allen Edmonds, Johnston & Murphy, and Alden all offer a genuine shell cordovan shoe. (You may be interested to know that cordovan leather comes from the hindquarters of a horse and is produced by only one company in America, located in Chicago, Illinois).

Polish cordovan shoes using cordovan polish for the body of the shoe, but use black polish in the creases of the leather, which tend to appear lighter with wear. If you are going to own a pair of genuine shell cordovan shoes, also buy yourself a cordovan-colored belt. Even better, if your finances permit, buy a genuine shell cordovan belt (available through the Ben Silver catalog).

If your taste (and budget) runs to "exotics," you can add either a pair of alligator or crocodile shoes to your collection. You should be aware of the difference, however. Alligator is more durable, and more expensive. You can distinguish alligator by its pattern of both squares and circles on the same skin. Crocodile, by contrast, is either all circles or all squares, never both together. Both kinds of shoes will run you a thousand dollars or more. As expensive as these are, they are considered a casual shoe.

If you are someone who is particularly hard to fit, then you may wish to seek out a maker of custom-made shoes (or perhaps you simply like things custom-made). There are a mere handful of places in the world that still make shoes to order. Four of the six are located in Europe, but fortunately there is one such bootmaker on the West Coast—Grisha's Custom Shoes in California—and one located on the East Coast—E. Vogel, Inc.—that can be found in lower Manhattan where they have been making shoes for well over one hundred years. The process starts with an appointment for a fitting and selection of a shoe style. They begin by making a wood last of your foot and from that they cut, sew, and glue the leather to form the shoe. A second fitting is required before they apply the sole to the shoes. Weeks of work later, you return a third time to slip into your new bespoke shoes. All this for about $1,300. When you consider that the price of John Lobb ready-made shoes can easily exceed that figure, this is a bargain.

When purchasing shoes, shop in the morning as your feet tend to swell as the day progresses. Always try shoes on wearing the kind of socks you will wear with that particular shoe. Don't try on loafers wearing athletic socks! If the shoe doesn't fit in the store, it probably won't fit any better when you get home. Your baseball glove needed to be broken in, shoes do not. Be sure to try on both shoes, not just the first one out of the shoe box.

For the same reason you want to own an umbrella to protect your clothing from wet conditons, you also want to own a pair of rubbers to protect your footwear in snow and slush. Rubbers will prevent moisture being absorbed into the soles of your shoes and the leather uppers will not get ruined or salt-stained. If you live in the snowbelt, you may want the kind of rubbers that cover your ankles. In Buffalo, you need the ones that go up to your knees.

Caring for Shoes

As you can see, having proper, quality shoes in your wardrobe represents a sizable investment. Your initial investment can carry you for many years, however, if you care for your shoes properly. Try not to wear the same pair of leather shoes two days in a row. Let them breathe and dry in cedar shoe trees that will absorb the moisture while maintaining the shape of the shoe. Never use plastic shoe trees, as they do not absorb moisture. Get in the habit of putting on your shoes with a shoehorn. Buy a two foot-long shoehorn and you don't even have to bend over to get your shoes on! And don't take your shoes off by levering the heel off one foot with the toe of the other.

Keep your shoes polished at all times. You could wear a $3,000 Oxford suit and still look unkempt if your shoes are scuffed, dull, or dirty. Polish your shoes with wax polish, as opposed to cream polish. Cream polish is easy to apply and works well with certain types of leathers, but it won't give you the same great shine that wax polish produces. It is a good idea to have a "shine sponge" handy—one at the office, another at home for times when you need to quickly restore the luster to your shoes. *Synovia* makes such a sponge—$5.00 at Nordstrom's among other places. This is not a substitute for polishing your shoes, but the shine sponge is great for touch-ups.

Following are tips on how best to polish your shoes:

- Always wet a paper towel with liquid soap and wipe the dirt off your shoes before polishing them. What good does it do to put polish over dirt?
- Polish your shoes with the shoe trees in, as you can get the polish into all the creases that way.
- Cover your index finger with several Band-Aids before polishing to avoid ending up with a stained finger.

- Apply the polish with a cotton cloth, then go over the shoes with the horsehair brush and buff them until they shine.
- Go over the shoes one more time with the cotton cloth to remove any remaining polish; this will avoid getting polish on the hem of your slacks.
- Between polishings, run a pair of nylons over the shoes to shine them up.
- Don't polish your shoes when they are wet.
- If all this strikes you as too much work, pay someone to shine them for you.

UNDERGARMENTS

Hosiery. What looks worse than socks that have slipped down around a man's ankles? Get used to wearing over-the-calf length socks, as they simply stay up better. Second choice is mid-calf length.

You will need several pairs of black socks and a pair each of navy, gray, and dark brown socks because your socks should match your trousers. If that is not possible, then your socks must match your shoes. A navy sock with a navy suit and black shoes is preferred over black socks. Gray slacks require gray socks. Remember: socks should be the color of your slacks or darker.

For casual wear, you can wear almost anything as long as it doesn't look garish. No white socks with casual slacks, however; wear the white ones with your athletic shoes. When you're wearing shorts, either don't wear any socks or wear golf socks. Don't wear "tennis" socks pulled up to your knee—you might as well be wearing a sign on your back that says, "DORK!"

Socks are available in 100 percent wool (Merino wool socks are divine), wool blend (85 percent wool, 15 percent nylon), cashmere, cotton, or silk. Buy some of each and see what you like better. Wool socks are best for warmth and absorption and thus are usually preferred. If and when you wear a tuxedo, the right sock is silk; yes, they make silk socks for men for formalwear. Socks are sized 1 ½ larger than shoes. If you wear a size 9 shoe, you need a 10½ size sock.

Throw away a sock with a hole in it because eventually Murphy's Law will catch up to you. You'll find yourself in a setting where you have to take your shoes off, only to be embarrassed by your holey socks. And don't keep the mate around, as it'll drive you crazy trying in vain to match up the pair.

In winter, you may experience your pant leg clinging to your socks, the result of static buildup caused by dry, heated air. The solution is simple: wet your hands with water and lightly rub them over your socks, and that will do the trick.

Be sure to wash dark socks with other dark clothes to avoid getting lint on your socks. Also clean the lint trap on your dryer regularly.

Undershirts. Long before you actually wear out a shirt, you may notice that the shirt has yellowed under the armpits from perspiration. When the yellow appears, ask your laundry to attack that area. If that doesn't work, throw the shirt away. The same goes for a frayed or yellowed collar. If you sweat profusely, or if you are extremely hairy, you may want to wear an undershirt beneath your dress shirt to protect the fabric and extend the life of the shirt. A crew neck undershirt is advised when you're wearing a shirt and tie. If you're wearing a sport shirt with the collar open, then wear a V-neck undershirt so it doesn't show at the neck. Avoid wearing the tank- or athletic-style undershirt, and under no circumstances should an undershirt display graphics on the front or back.

If you wear a V-neck sweater your best choice is a collared shirt underneath. For more casual occasions however, a colored crew neck undershirt beneath the sweater is acceptable.

Underwear. "Clean" is all that needs to be said for underwear. Whether it's boxers or briefs is your call; wear what's most comfortable to you. If you travel a good deal, you may want to buy 100 percent nylon boxers (Jockey makes them), as they take up very little room in your suitcase and you can wash them in your hotel room sink if need be. They dry quickly, particularly with a little help from a hair dryer.

POTPOURRI

Find a good tailor. They are worth every penny, as they can do anything from narrowing a tie, reversing a pleat, tapering a shirt, letting out a waistband, or mending a tear. My tailor is top-notch, and he is as important to me as my tax-preparer. Always make it a point to try on the item after the tailor has completed the work. Don't wait until you have reason to wear the item and find that the work was not to your satisfaction.

Pocket square. Not mandatory, but they do add an elegant touch to your suit or sport jacket. What you want to accomplish if you add a pocket square is a colorful complement to your tie. For example, if you are wearing a navy suit with a light blue shirt and a blue tie with a splash of red and white, then the pocket square should contain some of those same colors. Most are pure silk, but you also can buy linen or cotton pocket squares. The reason they are called pocket squares and not handkerchiefs is that squares are not meant for blowing your nose. Like ties, they are there simply for adornment and expression.

Learn how to present the item in the pocket by following the illustrations below. Don't have it sticking out of the pocket so far that the eye is drawn to it. Remember, it's an accent piece.

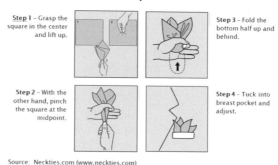

Step 1 – Grasp the square in the center and lift up.

Step 2 – With the other hand, pinch the square at the midpoint.

Step 3 – Fold the bottom half up and behind.

Step 4 – Tuck into breast pocket and adjust.

Source: Neckties.com (www.neckties.com)

More and more men's stores are carrying a nice selection of pocket squares, particularly Paul Stuart and Neiman Marcus. There is no standard size for pocket squares. I find anything larger than 14x14 inches to be too large to tuck into the breast pocket.

Collar stays. Plastic ones work fine, but brass collar stays are firmer. Don't leave home without them in your dress shirt, and don't leave them in your shirt while being laundered.

Cuff links. Cuff links set against French cuffs make for a very elegant look and thus are best worn with a suit. They are too dressy-looking for wear with a sport coat. You ought to own one set of cuff links, and matching studs, for wear with a tuxedo, and another pair for your dress shirts. One white and one blue shirt with French cuffs are more than adequate for most men. French cuffs have two drawbacks: they are difficult to put on, and they can't be worn under a sweater or without a jacket.

Suspenders. A belt will adequately hold up most men's trousers, but some men prefer wearing suspenders (or *braces*, as they are known in the apparel trade) because they like how suspenders look. If you are one of these men, be certain that your slacks have the required buttons inside the waistband for fastening the suspenders. Do not wear suspenders that clip to the waistband of your trousers. Suspenders need not match exactly with your tie, but they should not clash either. They simply need to complement the shirt and tie. If you wear suspenders, don't wear a belt, and vice versa.

Wallet. A conventional wallet worn in your back pocket eventually will wear a hole in your slacks. It also can cause discomfort from sitting on a bulging piece of leather stuffed with money, credit cards, and other items. Try carrying a breast-pocket style wallet instead.

Take it with you when you purchase a suit, and put it in the jacket's inside breast pocket so the tailor can adjust the button on the front of the suit to be even with the button hole on the other side (naturally, the weight of the wallet pulls that side of the jacket a touch lower than the other). I take it a step further and have the inside pocket lengthened (deepened) just a little, so the wallet sits under my breastbone and doesn't cause the jacket to bulge in front. Once you get in the habit of wearing a breast-pocket wallet, you may never go back to carrying one in your back pocket.

Some breast-pocket wallets come with a removable leather sleeve that holds your driver license and a couple credit cards. When not wearing a suit or jacket, you can carry the leather sleeve in your front pocket, along with a money clip for your cash. If you simply prefer a traditional wallet, keep it as thin as possible by taking out the old ballgame stubs, parking receipts, and other detritus. Keep a twenty-dollar bill inside for emergencies and carry your paper money in a money clip in your front trouser pocket.

Jewelry/Watches. Michael Jordan put a diamond earring in one earlobe back in the 1990s. As a result, today you see some men with three carats in each ear. It may fly in Hollywood and on the playing field, but it hasn't made it to the boardroom. The same can be said for pinky rings and thick neck and wrist chains. Keep jewelry in good taste: a wristwatch along with your collegiate ring is fine and a wedding ring where it applies. The chains can come out with your jeans but are best left in the drawer when suiting up.

Watches have become something of a fashion statement. Most men need two, maybe three watches at best. If you wear a suit every day you will want to wear a watch with either a metal or a leather band. The watch should not be so thick that you can't button the shirt cuff. For formal occasions, a thin elegant watch with a leather strap is more appropriate. Then you have the watch you wear with casual clothing or when playing sports, for which a rubber strap works well, as does a metal band

Shaving. If you ask men what one daily drudgery they would like to avoid, it would be shaving. Some men can get by without doing so, but most of us do the deed each and every day, like it or not. Here is one sure way to turn that daily unpleasantness into something pleasant: discard that can of shaving cream and adopt a new procedure.

It starts by acquiring a shaving brush (the best ones are made of badger hair), a jar of very rich shave cream from the likes of Truefitt & Hill or The Art of Shaving, a bottle of shaving oil, and a bottle of non-alcohol-based shaving balm. Admittedly this process adds several minutes to your morning routine, but you end up with a better shave, rarely a cut, and skin that feels so much better.

You begin by applying the shaving oil. Next, use the shaving brush to lather on the shave cream and then shave with your razor. Conclude with an application of the after-shave balm.

Truefitt & Hill (www.truefittandhill.com) has been in business for over two hundred years, supplying everything you need for a glorious shaving experience. Products from The Art of Shaving are made by Gillette and sold in finer department stores. Your annual cost of shaving will increase markedly, but once you engage in this process you might actually look forward to it.

Cologne/Aftershave.
Too much is awful; a little goes a long way. Bear in mind that what smells good on someone else may smell different on you. How do you know what smells good on you? If numerous people tell you that you smell good when wearing a particular fragrance, then you're probably wearing the right cologne, and more important, in the right amount.

Nose hair trimmer.
Buy one and use it periodically to ensure that you don't have hair growing out of your nose and ears. I have never yet heard a woman remark, "Gee, I love a man with lots of hair growing out of his nose."

Lint roller.
Keep one near where you dress—especially if you have a dog or a hairy wife. You also

should have a clothes brush to remove dust and enliven the fabric.

Dry Cleaning/Laundering. If you wear 100 percent cotton dress shirts (why would you wear anything else?) they need to be professionally laundered to look fresh. You, or your spouse, probably are not fond of ironing them anyway.

Cotton dress shirts look best if they get a shot of starch when laundered. There generally are three levels of starch: light, medium, and heavy. Heavy starch makes the shirt stand at attention but is too stiff for most people's taste, not to mention that your shirts will wear out that much faster. Light starch is okay for the body of the shirt, but the collar and cuffs could use a bit more. The solution: medium starch.

Be certain to remove the collar stays before having your shirts laundered. While dry cleaning is a necessity for cleaning many kinds of fabrics, the chemicals in dry cleaning do take their toll on clothing. If the item is not soiled or in need of pressing but only needs to be freshened up, the old tried and true method of hanging the item outdoors for a spell works wonders. This assumes, of course, that you don't live next to a coal plant and the neighbors don't make it a practice of stealing your garments.

Food stains. The quicker you act, the better the chance of removing food stains. Try scraping the food off first with a knife, and then rub the cloth against itself. If you have club soda handy, dab it on the stain with a clean cloth. Silk ties are especially susceptible to drips and spots. A quick solution is to dab the spot with a clean, white handkerchief or cloth and let dry. Later, use the small end of the tie to rub out the spot.

Winter storage. If you live in a climate that requires a seasonal change in apparel, then you should know how to store your clothes. The first order of business is to make certain your closet is clean. Vacuuming to get out dust mites and moth sacs is recommended. Lose the wire hangers—they are no good for hanging any heavy item of apparel. Use wood hangers for everything except shirts. Don't store your garments in the plastic bags that come from the laundry. Clothes need to breathe. Make certain your clothes are kept in a dry area. Basements are not a good choice, as the moisture in basements can promote mildew and odors. Be mindful of bugs, which love cardboard boxes. Keep your wool items in polypropylene clothing bags, as insects won't bore through them.

Full-length mirror. You should have a full-length mirror in your bedroom so that when you finish dressing, you can take a look to see that everything is right before going off into the world. At the very least, it will save you the embarrassment of leaving home with your fly open.

Catalogs. There are scores of men's clothing catalogs—too many, to be sure. Four very good ones include Bullock & Jones (www.bullockandjones.

com), Paul Stuart (www.paulstuart.com), Maus & Hoffman (www.mausandhoffman.com), and Carroll & Co. (www.carrollandco.com). All four put out numerous catalogs per year of very good quality, primarily casual merchandise.

Salespeople. If you make it a point to shop consistently at select stores, you normally will find a salesperson who can be helpful in building your wardrobe. Ask him or her to call you when certain merchandise arrives that you like. A good salesperson can put you on to upcoming sales, make it easier for you to return merchandise, and see to it that the best tailor always attends to you (very important).

BUILDING YOUR WARDROBE

*I*f you are serious about putting together a truly outstanding wardrobe, it will likely take you several years, many thousands of dollars, some careful shopping, and proper planning. Start by taking an inventory of what you own (by category). Decide what pieces fit you well, which of those items you like to wear, and what looks good on you. As a general rule, if you have not worn a particular item in the past three years, you probably never will—so give it away. If your partner tells you that something doesn't look good on you, it probably doesn't—give it away.

Next, take a look at items that may need alteration or repair and attend to them. Then, decide on which items you need to fill in the gaps, perhaps a navy blue suit, a pair of genuine shell cordovan shoes, or a good raincoat, and plan for those purchases by adding a few items each year. There is nothing wrong with telling your spouse what item(s) you would like for Father's Day, Christmas, birthdays, etc. that will help accomplish your goal.

Take note of what brands you prefer, and when they go on sale (everything in menswear goes on sale at least yearly). Also take into consideration your personality, the industry in which you work, your leisure activities, and your geography. There are certain patterns, styles, and colors that you can wear if you work in the fashion or entertainment industry in New York or LA that just won't fly in the boardroom in Chicago. All these factors should play a role in your clothing choices. If you go about this task in a thoughtful manner, you will surely see a marked improvement in your wardrobe.

The (Basic) Men's Business Wardrobe
- Navy blue solid
- Gray solid
- Gray chalk stripe
- Navy blue stripe
- Gray herringbone (optional)
- Gray or navy blue pin dot suit (optional)

One or Two Sport Jackets
- Navy blue wool or cashmere
- *Either* a tweed for winter,

- *Or a* combination wool/silk/linen

Several Wool Flannel or Gabardine Solid-Color Dress Slacks

- Navy
- Black
- Tan
- Medium gray
- Dark gray
- Brown

Twelve to Fifteen Dress Shirts

- Two white with spread collars
- One blue with spread collar
- One blue button-down
- One pink with any style collar
- One ecru with any style collar
- One white with blue stripe with any style collar

Several Belts

- One black with a gold buckle
- One black with a silver buckle
- One brown with gold buckle
- One black braid
- One fabric belt for casual slacks

A Dozen or More Ties

- At least one red/blue/white stripe
- One red pin dot or polka dot
- A few blue regimental ties
- A gray/silver/black foulard or stripe
- A few colorful foulards

Four or More Pairs of Shoes

- A black lace oxford or wing-tip
- A black slip-on
- A cordovan tassel
- A brown lace oxford or wing-tip

Two Overcoats

- One tan raincoat
- One wool or cashmere navy, gray, or black top coat

Two or Three Sweaters for Business Casual Wear

- A navy blue V-neck
- A gray mock turtleneck
- A maroon crewneck

Six or More Pairs of Dress Socks

- Black
- Dark grey
- Navy blue
- Brown

CONCLUSION

*D*oes any of this really matter? Well, you do have to get dressed every morning, and it certainly doesn't hurt to look nice. People form an opinion of you in an instant, and how you look plays a part in their perception of you.

Dressing smartly is both an acquired skill and a worthy goal, which can be attained with a modicum of effort. At the very least, don't look like you sleep in your clothes, or wear clothes that are soiled or don't fit. If you have the choice of being "over-dressed" for an occasion or "under-dressed," choose over-dressed every time. You will never be embarrassed, and you'll never feel compelled to apologize. Clothes don't make the man, but looking good should at the very least make you feel good about yourself, as well as help you make a good impression.

Having said all this, I fully appreciate that there are scores of people whose jobs and lifestyles do not require that they wear a suit, nor do they care if they ever own a cashmere V-neck sweater. If you are one of those who can get by with a good dog and a pair of jeans, God love you. You might just wash the dog and the jeans on occasion…

SELECTED PURVEYORS OF MEN'S CLOTHING

Purveyor	Description	Web Site
Ben Silver	Catalog company—good place for blazer buttons and cuff links.	bensilver.com
Bullock & Jones	Catalog company—large selection of wonderful casual apparel.	bullockandjones.com
Burberry	A great raincoat; beautiful ties, too.	burberry.com
Carrol & Co.	A few retail stores; good catalog of casual apparel.	carrollandco.com
Jos. A. Bank	For those who need a size 44 suit jacket and 32-inch slacks; moderately priced apparel.	josbank.com
Loro Piana	The finest outerwear anywhere, with a dozen stores in the United States.	loropiana.com
Maus & Hoffman	A few retail stores; good catalog of casual apparel.	mausandhoffman.com
Neiman Marcus	A fabulous tie selection; John Lobb shoes.	neimanmarcus.com
Nordstrom	Great shoe selection; exclusive Faconnable brand of great casual clothes.	nordstrom.com
Paul Stuart	Good selection of pocket squares and colorful socks; wonderful sweaters, too.	paulstuart.com
Regent Tailor	Hong Kong custom tailors—they visit major U.S. cities yearly.	regentcustomtailor@ hotmail.com
Tom James Co.	Clothes that come to you; custom-made apparel.	tomjames.com

These selections are totally my own. No monies or other remuneration were received from these businesses in return for mention in this publication.

FORTY-FIVE TIPS FOR DRESSING WELL

1. Your dress shirts should be professionally laundered and contain starch, particularly in the collar and cuffs.
2. Don't wear a button-down collar shirt with a suit, nor with a double-breasted jacket.
3. Never button the bottom button on a suit jacket, but always button the one above it.
4. Always have your suit or sport jacket buttoned when standing.
5. Don't wear a patterned suit with a patterned shirt and a patterned tie—it's just too much for most men to coordinate properly.
6. Don't buy slacks with an English pleat.
7. Don't tuck your tie into the waistband of your trousers.

8. Don't buy cheap, thin 1-ply cashmere sweaters.
9. When tied, your tie should be no shorter than the top of your belt buckle and no longer than the bottom.
10. Don't bother with wool or cotton ties—the knot will always look lousy.
11. Ditch the tie clasps and pins.
12. Use collar stays in your dress shirts.
13. Wear silk socks with a tuxedo.
14. Don't wear socks with sandals.
15. Your socks should be the same color as your slacks.
16. If you must own a white belt, wear it golfing and nowhere else.
17. If you wear suspenders, don't wear a belt too.
18. If you wear an undershirt under an open-collared shirt, then wear a V-neck undershirt and not a crew neck T-shirt.
19. If you're heavy-set, don't wear anything with horizontal stripes.
20. Keep cedar wood shoe trees in your shoes.
21. Wear over-the-calf socks.
22. Learn to put a dimple in your tie.
23. Remove your tie by reversing the process.
24. Alternate putting on your belt—left to right one day, right to left the next day—to keep it from "bowing."

25. If you can't button your suit jacket, don't wear it.
26. No cowboy boots with a suit—not even in Amarillo.
27. If you wear a vest, leave the bottom button unbuttoned.
28. Don't wear a button-down collared shirt with a bow tie.
29. When wearing a tuxedo, wear a wing-collared shirt and be sure the "wings" are behind the bow tie.
30. Shoes should be darker than your suit.
31. Always keep an extra pair of shoelaces on hand.
32. Don't wear a raincoat over a tuxedo.
33. Don't wear a car coat over a suit—wear a topcoat or trench coat.
34. Always use a shoehorn to put on your shoes.
35. If the pleats on your trouser are splayed or there is a horizontal crease running across the fly, your trousers are too snug.
36. Never dress more casually than your client.
37. Never wear a blazer or sport coat to a job interview.
38. Don't wear the same pair of shoes two days in a row—give them a day to dry.
39. Your dress shirt should be a lighter color than your suit.
40. Don't wear light colored socks with a suit.
41. Don't polish your shoes when they are wet.

42. When purchasing shoes, try on both shoes.
43. Don't wear suede shoes, shoes with a rubber sole, moccasins, or topsiders with a suit.
44. When traveling, pack your silk tie(s) in a leather case or plastic canister.
45. Your belt should be the same color as your shoes.